More than a Splatball Game!

Squaring off with the giants in your life

CHECK OUT ALL THESE
★ GOLD NUGGET GUIDES ★

God Rocks!

More than a
Splatball Game!

Standard
PUBLISHING
CINCINNATI, OHIO

Squaring off with the
giants in your life

Published by Standard Publishing, Cincinnati, Ohio. A division of Standex International Corporation. Printed in Italy.

Written by Lise Caldwell. Art by Chelsea Road Productions, Inc. Project editor: Robin Stanley. Art direction and design: Rule29. Cover design: Rule29. Production: settingPace.

ISBN 0-7847-1457-6

09 08 07 06 05 04 03   9 8 7 6 5 4 3 2 1

More than a Splatball Game!

CONTENTS

WELCOME TO ROCKY RIDGE . . .

. . . The splatball capital of the world! A bit like baseball, but much messier, splatball is the favorite game of Chip Livingstone and his friends. Their team, the Rocky Ridge Rockets, makes the stadium ROCK with one boink run after another! During splatball season, everyone in town plays a part in helping out the team. Mrs. Crag stands in behind the plate, calling strikes and splats. Deacon Dug offers his expertise on the base paths, telling runners when to hold up and when to go home. Big B, the local radio personality, announces play by play from high atop his perch in the press booth. And the coach of the Rockets is none other than Bullseye! He's the most famous of all splatball pitchers— a legend and a God Rock hero—who teaches his team a lot about life both on and off the splatball field.

Chip, Gem, Splinter, Carb, Kitney, and others have a great time at the academy, at Stone Church, and at splatball. But they all know that there are some BIG problems in Rocky Ridge. And part of being a young rock is learning how to face those problems.

With the help of Bullseye, Mrs. Crag, and others, most problems in Rocky Ridge get worked out . . . eventually. But along the way, everyone learns that God Rocks!

So come along and get to know The God Rocks!, their heroes, and their friends a little better. You'll have a rockin' good time!

AN OVERVIEW OF
SPLATBALL SQUARE-OFF

The splatball championships are coming up and the Rocky Ridge Rockets are sure they'll have no problem beating the Granitville Giants, whom Chip jokingly calls "Grannies."

Kitney Stoon faces a giant of her own when some of the "cool" rock chicks at the academy call her "cute" and make fun of her "dipsy-do-bob" hair. "Cute" is definitely not "cool" and Kitney is as low as low can go, until Gem picks her up with some friendly— and godly—advice!

When Kitney becomes a last-minute sub for the championship splatball game, things start looking up—for Kitney AND the team. But then Chip sends Ruff on a spy mission and discovers that the "Grannies" have a GIANT secret weapon! Now the Rockets are shaking in their shoes!

With their ace, Org, leading the way, the Granitville Giants begin to clobber the Rockets in the championship game. But the Rockets have an ace of their own—Bullseye, a coach who is a God Rock hero! He tells the story of when he came face-to-face with Goliath and inspires the Rockets to rely on someone even bigger than the Granitville pitcher.

How can you face the giants in *your* life?
Look here and find out!

Crack open the pages of this book and get ready for a rockin' good time, as Chip Livingstone and his friends learn that God is bigger than any problem, no matter *how* big!

Remember the story of David and Goliath? Bullseye, Chip's splatball coach, does because he was there. He was the rock David used to bop Goliath with God's help. David had faith that God would help him defeat the giant, and he did! Because of his face-to-face encounter with Goliath, Bullseye knows that giants are never quite as big as they seem, especially when God is on your side!

Each chapter in this book tells a story about The God Rocks! and how they rely on God to help them through their giant problems. In each story you'll also find . . .

* Thinkin' It Through—questions to help you think about the main point of the story

* Bullseye's On-Target Talk—good advice from the rock who bopped Goliath
* Set in Stone: Bullseye's Memory Verse—a special Bible verse for you to remember
* Get Rockin'—great ideas for defeating your own giants with God's help, including some space for writing down your thoughts

If you want, you can read a little bit of each chapter every day so you'll have plenty of time to think about the story, answer the questions, learn the verse, and start defeating your giants. Or read a chapter all at once! Whatever you do, have a great time learning that no giant is ever as big as it seems when God is on your side!

CHAPTER 1

SPLINTER STICKS OUT

Do not conform any longer to the pattern of this world, but be transformed by the renewing of your mind. Romans 12:2

"**C**hip, I'll trade you a Diamond Back for a Craggy Comet," Carb said one day during lunch.

"Is that a fair trade?" Chip asked. "My Comet is worth ten of your Diamond Backs."

Just then Splinter walked up. "Are you rocks talking about your Monster Moss trading cards again?" he asked.

"Come on, Splinter," Chip said. "These cards are spikin'. You just don't know what you're missing."

"No, I guess I don't," Splinter said. He decided to go sit with Gem and Kitney.

"Have a seat," Gem said. "We were just opening up a pack of Monster Moss Cards!"

"Splinter, where are your cards?" Kitney asked.

"I don't have any," he said, setting his lunch tray down. "I'm not interested in Monster Moss stuff."

"What?!" they said together. "All the rocks in school have them," added Kitney.

"Since I don't have any, I guess that's not totally true," Splinter said, and started to sit down. Gem and Kitney gave each other a "secret" look. Kitney said, "Splinter, you're welcome to sit here, but we're just going to be talking about Monster Moss."

"Yeah," Gem said, handing him back his tray. "You'll probably just be bored."

Splinter walked away to eat his lunch alone. He didn't get it. What was the big deal about Monster Moss Trading Cards, anyway? And why did it bother everyone that he didn't like them?

Splinter spent the next few days alone, but he couldn't go anywhere without hearing about Monster Moss. The only time no one talked about it was during class, but Splinter knew the other rocks were passing notes and making trades when Mrs. Crag's back was turned.

"Why don't you get into Monster Moss?" Chip asked. "All the other rocks are."

"I know," said Splinter. "But just because everyone else likes something doesn't mean I have to like it!"

"But WHY don't you like it?" Carb asked.

"Because it's DUMB!" Splinter yelled. Right away he knew he'd said the wrong thing. Carb turned red, and Chip looked really angry.

"Look, Splinter," Chip said. "Until you want to talk to us about Monster Moss, maybe you just shouldn't talk to us at all."

"Maybe you're right!"

That afternoon, Splinter went to see Deacon Dug. He had to talk to someone! But when he walked into the Deacon's office . . .

"What are you doing?" Splinter asked, almost yelling.

"I'm just looking through some Monster Moss cards," Deacon Dug said.

"Not you too?!" Splinter moaned.

"What's the matter?"

"It's just that all the rocks at school are collecting those cards, and because I'm NOT collecting them, no one wants to talk to me!" Splinter said.

"Why don't you like Monster Moss?" Dug asked.

"Because it seems kind of silly," Splinter said nervously.

"I couldn't agree more," Deacon Dug said. "I asked Gem to let me see her cards—she hasn't talked about anything else lately—and they are kind of goofy."

Splinter looked relieved. "I just hate that everyone is mad at me because I don't like the cards. I don't want to feel like I have to like everything my friends like just so they'll like me."

"Good friends shouldn't be that way, but even good friends aren't perfect," said Dug. "Your friends may feel that you think

THEY are silly because you think the cards are silly."

"What can I do?" Splinter asked.

"Well, you could start collecting the cards so you can be just like everyone else," Dug said. "I don't think that's the best choice, though. What you *can* do is make sure your friends know that you like *them.*"

"But they should KNOW that!"

"Maybe they're not so sure. Just give it a try," said Dug.

That night, Splinter went to Chip's house. "I'm sorry I yelled," Splinter said. "I really want to hang out with you—with everybody. But I don't want to talk about Monster Moss all the time."

"That's alright, Splinter," Chip said. "I was getting pretty tired of Monster Moss anyway. Wanna hear a sparkin' new song I've been working on?"

The two friends grinned as Chip kicked into the groove of his new song.

Thinkin' It Through!

* Why do you think Splinter's friends wanted him to be interested in what they were interested in?

* What fads or trends do you know about right now?

* What do you think about those fads?

BULLSEYE'S ON-TARGET TALK

★ **PLEASE GOD:** Don't follow the crowd!

What do you think it means to be "cool"? With friends, being cool usually means being interested in the same things everyone else likes and not wanting to be different from anyone else. Being cool means that everyone likes you and looks up to you, right?

Sometimes trying to be cool or popular leads kids into choices that aren't best for them. Those choices can be something small—like pretending to be interested in something you think is silly. But those choices can be very serious—like feeling pressured to drink alcohol or smoke or shoplift. The thing is, if you are more concerned about what your friends think of you than about what you think of yourself, or what God thinks of you, then chances are you're going to do things you don't feel good about.

Splinter made a good choice. There might not be anything wrong with trading cards, but it's wrong to pretend to like something you don't like just so your friends will accept you. For a while, he felt pretty lonely. When you choose not to go along with the crowd, you might feel lonely, too.

But in the end, Splinter's friends respected him more for standing up for himself, even over a little thing like trading cards. Don't conform yourself to what this world tells you that you ought to do. But obey God and please him, even when doing so might not please the people around you.

SET IN STONE: Bullseye's Memory Verse

Live in order to please God.

1 Thessalonians 4:1

GET ROCKIN'
WANT TO BRING DOWN THE PEER PRESSURE GIANT? HERE'S HOW!

✱ The next time you want to buy something or do something, ask yourself, "Why?" Is it because you really want to? Or is it because you think your friends will like you more if you do?

✱ Find something that you really enjoy doing all by yourself. People who are scared of being alone are much more likely to do things just to get friends, but those kinds of friends usually don't last.

✱ Read Philippians 4:8. This verse describes the kinds of things that are pleasing to God. When you are deciding what to do with your time, think about this verse.

CHAPTER 2

_____

_____

_____

_____

_____

THE SPLATBALL NATURAL

*All of you, clothe yourselves with humility toward one another,
because, "God opposes the proud but gives grace to the humble."*
1 Peter 5:5

"**S**pikin'! The splatball trophy is MINE!" Chip yelled.

"Chip, it was a great practice," Coach Bullseye said. "But I wouldn't go grabbing for that splatball trophy just yet, son."

"Yeah, Chip, it takes all of us to win a game of splatball," Kitney added.

"But you couldn't do it without the greatest splatball pitcher ever known."

"Take it easy, there, sport," said Gem.

"I may not be the greatest yet," Chip said quietly, gazing at the empty bleachers, "but I will be. And *someday* the fans will be chanting *my* name!"

The next day at school, Chip saw Twinkee and Crystal, the most popular rocks at school. "Hi, Chip!" Twinkee said. "How was practice?"

"Great!" Chip said. "I was rockin'!"

"Would you like to sit with us at lunch today?" Crystal asked.

"Um," Chip always ate lunch with Carb and Splinter, but he said, "Yeah, sure."

"We'd just love to hear all about splatball," Crystal said.

"Yeah, and you're the best rock in the world to tell us," Twinkee added.

Chip went home feeling pretty good about himself. When he walked in the door, his mom said, "Chip, would you please take out the garbage?"

"Make Nuggie do it, Mom," he answered. "I can't be bothered with stuff like that." And he went to his room. Ruby tried to call him back, but Chip was too busy thinking about splatball to hear her.

Ruff was waiting for him. They always played together when Chip got home from school. But today, Chip wasn't in the mood. All he wanted to do was dream about splatball greatness. "Not now, Ruff!" Ruff just hung his head and went away sad.

When Chip got to school the next day, Twinkee and Crystal caught up with him. "We just couldn't wait to hear more about splatball!" they said. Chip was excited, but he did wonder why they were suddenly so interested in sports.

That afternoon was another great practice for Chip. OK, so maybe he threw a couple of bad pitches. And maybe he got splatted out a couple of times. But still . . .

After practice, Gem went to see Coach Bullseye. "I'm worried about Chip," she said. "He's always been a good player, but lately

Did You Know

Hitting the soft side of a **SPLATBALL** will leave you splattered with mustard, slime, . . . or worse!

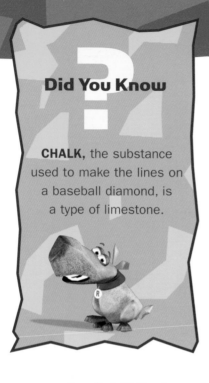
he just brags about how good he is. We're all getting tired of it."

"I think I know why Chip's had a little pride problem lately," the coach said.

"Seems more like a BIG pride problem to me," Gem muttered as she walked away.

The day of the next game, Chip felt like he was the biggest boulder in the world. *I can beat anyone!* he thought. Then he saw something very strange.

"Crystal! Twinkee! What are you doing on the field? You're not playing splatball, are you?" he asked.

"As if we'd play that messy sport," said Crystal.

"We're the new splatball cheerleaders!" Twinkee said.

"I didn't know there were cheerleaders in splatball!" Chip said.

"There are now, thanks to you," Crystal said.

"We've wanted to be cheerleaders for a long time," said Twinkee. "But Coach Bullseye always said the Rockets didn't need cheerleaders. After we learned all about splatball from you, though, we convinced him!"

Chip started to get it. "You mean, you were just trying to get information from me?"

"Yep!"

"So you don't think I'm the greatest splatball player ever?"

"Nope," said the rock chicks. "Now get out of the way. You're blocking the crowd's view of us."

Chip felt really stupid. And he'd been so rude to the other rocks on his team. "I've got to go apologize."

"What's that, Chip?" Coach Bullseye asked, overhearing Chip's conversation.

Chip told him about what happened with Crystal and Twinkee.

"I thought maybe something like that was going on," said Coach. "It's easy to get caught up in what other people say about us. But the best thing to do is to remember that everything we're good at is from God."

"I'm really sorry about my attitude," Chip said.

"You are a good splatball pitcher," Coach Bullseye said. "But you're not the greatest ever."

"I'm not?"

"Nope," said Coach with a wink. "I am!"

Thinkin' It Through!

* Why did Chip start to think he was such a great splatball player?

* What did Coach Bullseye tell him?

* What would you have said to Chip if he were one of your friends?

BULLSEYE'S ON-TARGET TALK

★ **BE LIKE JESUS:** Humble yourself!

God has given each person talents, gifts, and abilities. There is nothing wrong with wanting to use our abilities or being glad that we have them. But when we forget that all those good gifts come from God and start thinking we are the greatest thing ever, we've got a pride problem.

We run into trouble when we begin to compare our gifts to someone else's. It's OK to think, "I can sing well. I'm glad God gave me a good singing voice." It's a problem when you start thinking, "I can sing better than my sister, my best friend, and everyone else I know—I must be better than them!" When we compare the gifts God gave us with the gifts he has given to other people, we run into two big problems: jealousy and pride. Jealousy is when you think someone else is better than you and that makes you mad; pride is when you think you are better than someone else and that makes you glad.

The thing is, we shouldn't compare ourselves to others. We should compare ourselves with Christ's example. He is God's Son and the Creator of the Universe, but he didn't come to earth and say, "Look at me. I sure am a lot better than all you awful people." Instead, he served people and loved people. Our attitudes should be like Christ's.

SET IN STONE: Bullseye's Memory Verse

Your attitude should be the same as that of Christ Jesus.

Philippians 2:5

GET ROCKIN'
NEED TO STAND UP AGAINST THE PRIDE GIANT? START HERE!

✸ Make a list of the things you are good at. Thank God at least once a week for giving you those abilities.

✸ Start reading through one of the books that tells the story of Jesus' life. These books are called the Gospels: Matthew, Mark, Luke, and John. You'll see habits of humility that Jesus lived out. Make note of the habits you want to start developing.

✸ Read Philippians 2:1–11 to get another idea of the way Jesus lived a humble life.

CHAPTER 3

_____

_____

_____

_____

_____

A FROG IN GEM'S THROAT

Do not be anxious about anything. Philippians 4:6

Gem was walking down the hall to her locker when she spotted it. The sign said, "Lapis Lazuli Vocal Music Summer Workshop Auditions Saturday." Gem felt her heart race. Ever since she was a pebble, she's dreamed of going to the Lazuli workshop. All the really great rock singers had gone. Lapis herself was supposed to be a bit . . . odd. Gem had heard rumors that Lapis made rocks sing while standing on their heads! This was the first year that Gem was old enough to audition for the summer program.

"Watch out!" Chip yelled, as Gem walked straight into him, knocking all of their books to the ground. "Gem, are you OK?"

"I, I . . ." Gem shook her head. She couldn't even talk. She just pointed to the poster.

"Oh, I see," Chip said. "Nervous about the Lazuli audition? You'll be fine."

But Gem didn't feel fine. Her stomach felt all twisted up and her mouth felt dry. Worst of all, she couldn't stop shaking, making it hard for her to walk.

After school, she went to the music room to practice her songs for the audition. After a few minutes, Mrs. Crag came in. "What are you working on, Gem, your Lazuli audition pieces?" Mrs. Crag asked.

Gem said, "Yes, ma'am. Mrs. Crag, I'm so nervous! What do you know about Lapis Lazuli? Is she really as crazy as people say?"

"She is a bit strange," Mrs. Crag said. "Why, at my audition, she made me hold a frog in my hand while I sang."

"Why?" Gem asked.

"She said if there was a frog in my hand, it couldn't be in my throat!" Mrs. Crag laughed. "Don't worry, Gem. You'll be fine."

"Why does everyone keep saying that?" Gem wondered. She slept very little that week and ate even less. She sang so much she began to lose her voice. "Maybe if I could hold a horse in my hand," she thought, "I wouldn't sound so hoarse!"

Finally the day of the audition came. Gem woke early. She didn't touch her breakfast. Her father, Deacon Dug, looked at her with concern. "Sugar rock," he said, "do you think maybe you're making too big of a deal out of this audition?"

Did You Know

When she isn't busy singing or writing songs, **GEM** enjoys doing community outreach with her dad.

Did You Know

Birds often eat tiny little **STONES** to help them digest the food they eat.

"Dad, don't you understand? This is the biggest thing that has ever happened to me! This is my chance to be a star! If I don't make it, my life might as well be over."

She ran out of the house. She'd never felt more nervous in her life!

The auditions were crowded with singers. Each of them was given a number and a place in line. After what seemed like forever, it was finally Gem's turn. She stepped to the middle of the stage, opened her mouth, and . . . nothing happened. No sound came out. What was wrong?

From the back of the auditorium, she heard Miss Lazuli shout, "FROG!" One of her assistants ran out and handed a frog to Gem. The frog felt slimy, and it wriggled around in her hands. Gem started to giggle. She could barely hold on to the wriggling creature. Once more Miss Lazuli's voice came from the back of the auditorium. This time she shouted, "Sing!" And a very strange thing happened. Gem was so focused on the frog, she forgot to be nervous. And she sang—and sang. When she told her dad about it that night, she said, "Dad, I think I sang better than I ever have before! I don't know if I got in or not, but I did my best. Why did I freeze up like that, though?"

"Everyone gets nervous sometimes, Gem," Dug said. "But you can always remember that God is in control. He tells us not to be afraid."

"What do you do when you get nervous, Dad?" Gem asked.

"I tell myself that I need to be still and know that God is God," he said.

Thinkin' It Through!

* What made this audition such a big deal for Gem?

* Do you think holding a frog would have made you less nervous?

* What do you get nervous about?

BULLSEYE'S ON-TARGET TALK

★ **TALK TO GOD:** He cares about you!

Being anxious or nervous is pretty common. Some people get anxious before tests, when they speak in public, or when meeting new people. If almost everyone gets anxious, why does the Bible tell us not to get anxious about anything? If you read that verse, you need to read the whole thing: "Do not be anxious about anything, but in everything, by prayer and petition, with thanksgiving, present your requests to God. And the peace of God, which transcends all understanding, will guard your hearts and minds in Christ Jesus" (Philippians 4:6, 7).

OK, I know that's got some big words and hard ideas in it. But basically what that verse is saying is that when you feel nervous or anxious, talk to God about it. Ask him for help. Thank him for his comfort. And he can give your heart and mind a special peace that other people may not be able to understand. What a great promise!

Really, what you need to remember is that God is in control. Even if you fail a test or mess up a speech, God is still in control. He will always love you, no matter what you do. So relax in the peace that he gives!

SET IN STONE: Bullseye's Memory Verse

Cast all your anxiety on [God] because he cares for you.

1 Peter 5:7

GET ROCKIN'
HERE ARE SOME WAYS TO CALM THE ANXIETY GIANT!

✷ What are you nervous about right now? Talk to God about it!

✷ Think of ways to help yourself through nervous situations. Do you need to be sure to study really well for your test? Then do it!

✷ Whenever you feel nervous, think about all the people in your life who love you, no matter what. And know that God loves you more than all of them.

CHAPTER 4

_____

_____

_____

_____

_____

ALONE-A-THON

To you, O Lord, I lift up my soul. . . . Turn to me and be gracious to me, for I am lonely and afflicted. Psalm 25:1, 16

The annual Rocky Ridge Rockathon was just around the corner, and the whole town was excited. "Everyone will be there!" Gem told Chip and Carb. "And this is the first year we are all old enough to be rockers."

"Yeah, last year all they let me do was sit at the score table," said Chip.

"I had to bring everyone drinks and snacks!" Gem said.

Carb didn't say anything.

The Rockathon was a town tradition.

All night long, the rocks rocked! Literally. They all competed to see how long they could keep rocking in a rocking chair! The Rockathon helped raise money for the Academy. All the rocks in school were supposed to help. The older ones got to compete, and this year's prize was a trip to Stony Acres Rock Resort. There was lots of good food and great games—it was the biggest event of the school year. Only . . .

"I can't go," Carb said.

"What?!" yelled Chip and Gem at the same time.

"My mom says I have to stay home that night. I have to rock-sit my little sister."

"But it's the Rockathon!" Gem said.

"Everyone will be there!" Chip said.

"Everyone but me," Carb said.

The next few days at school, the Rockathon was all anyone talked about. The girls talked about what they would wear; the boys bragged about how long they could rock. But Carb stayed pretty quiet. And he felt totally alone.

Finally the big day came. All the students were excused from class to help decorate the gym. Chip, Gem, and Splinter worked hard making everything look just right.

Gem saw Carb sitting on the bleachers. "Chip," she said, "why don't you go try to cheer Carb up."

Chip sat next to Carb. Chip told him all his best jokes. He offered him some marble chips. He even started to bark like Ruff. He got some strange looks from a few other rocks, but Carb hardly seemed to notice. Finally Carb said, "I know what you're doing, Chip. Thanks. But I'd rather just be by myself—I need to get used to it."

That night, after his sister fell asleep, Carb sat at home all alone. He thought about how much fun everyone was having without him. *They're probably not even thinking about me.*

When his mom got home, she came in to say goodnight. "You're really down about missing the Rockathon, aren't you, Carb?" she asked.

"Aw, Mom," he said. "I know you needed me to stay home. But right now I feel like the loneliest rock in the world."

"I understand, Carb," his mom said. "I really do. When I was your age, my ride for the Rockathon forgot me, and I didn't get to go."

"If you knew how important it was to me," Carb asked, "why didn't you let me go?"

"Carb, I really did need you to stay home tonight," his mom said. "But maybe it's even more important for you to learn what I learned."

"What's that?" Carb asked.

"That you can't always be with your friends. Things happen. And you have to learn to be happy being just with you—and God."

"Alone with God?" Carb asked. "What do you mean?"

Carb's mom told him that even though being without your friends seems like a giant problem, you can really talk to God and learn about him when no one else is around.

"God gives us friends," she said. "But he also gives us time away from them to be with him."

After his mom said goodnight, Carb thought about what she'd said. Maybe missing the Rockathon wasn't the end of the world. Carb still felt a little lonely, but this time he talked to God about it. And before long, he felt much better.

! **Thinkin' It Through!**

⁎ Why did Carb feel so lonely?

⁎ What made Carb feel better?

⁎ How can you feel better when you are lonely?

BULLSEYE'S ON-TARGET TALK

★ GOD IS WITH YOU: You're never alone!

Everyone feels lonely sometimes. Maybe you've had a time when you couldn't go somewhere with all your friends. Or maybe you've had times when you didn't feel like you had any friends. It's hard to feel left out, and sometimes it just seems boring to be alone.

Have you ever heard people say that they feel most alone in a crowd? Even when you're around lots of other people, you can feel lonely if no one is paying any attention to you.

One way to cut down on loneliness is to be a good friend. Be kind to others and show interest in them and their lives, and you'll have lots of great people to spend time with.

But no matter what, there are times when you will be alone. And that's a good thing. It's hard to do things like pray, read the Bible, or think about anything (like homework!) when you're with a bunch of people.

Being alone doesn't mean you have to feel lonely. You can remember God's promise to always be with you. In the Bible (Hebrews 13:5) God says He is the One who will never leave you or ignore you. Talk to him when you feel lonely and enjoy your one-on-one time with God!

SET IN STONE: Bullseye's Memory Verse

God has said, "Never will I leave you; never will I forsake you."

Hebrews 13:5

GET ROCKIN'
SQUARING OFF WITH THE
LONELINESS GIANT? START HERE!

✶ The next time you're with a group at school or church, look for someone else who might be feeling lonely. Try to include that person in your conversations, too.

✶ Start a journal. Write in it when you feel lonely. Talk to God about how you feel and what is going on in your life.

✶ When you feel lonely, write a story or paint a picture about how you feel. Later, look at it again and think about how your feelings have changed. Remember that no one feeling lasts forever, even the feeling of loneliness.

CHAPTER 5

A CHIP ON HIS SHOULDER

Refrain from anger and turn from wrath. Psalm 37:8

"**D**ad, Nuggie forgot to feed Ruff *again!*" Chip yelled as he stomped into the living room.

"Isn't feeding Ruff your job, Chip?" Cliff asked.

"But Nuggie said she'd do it! She makes me so mad some-times. She acts like—like a little pebble!"

"Chip, Nuggie *is* still a young pebble. Try not to be so hard on her," Cliff said.

But Chip was still angry. Lately he found himself getting mad at everyone. Last week, Gem forgot a rehearsal, and Chip yelled at her for twenty minutes. Splinter was late for a study session, so Chip packed up his books and stormed out. *What's wrong with me?* Chip wondered.

Later that afternoon, he saw Carb at the ice cream cave. "Hey, what's rollin', Chip?" Carb asked.

"It's been better," Chip answered. He didn't feel like talking about how mad he felt, so he changed the subject. "What's the special today?" he asked.

"Sediment Sundaes!" Carb answered. "Want me to order you one? My treat!"

"Sure," said Chip. Then he added, to himself, "It's about time you paid for something."

"What did you say, Chip?" Carb asked.

"Nothing," Chip said.

"Hey, Chip, I've been meaning to ask you—do you think you could help me with my research project for Mrs. Crag?"

"Is that why you got me a sundae?" Chip asked. "You just wanted me to do your work for you!"

"That's not it at all, Chip," Carb said. "It's just that Gem was busy, and . . ."

"Oh, so I wasn't even your first choice?" Chip started to raise his voice.

"What's wrong with you, Chip?" Carb asked. "Why are you getting so angry?"

"Because I can't stand being around rocks like you!" Chip yelled. Everyone in the ice cream shop stared at them. Chip stomped out.

Carb looked pretty hurt. He didn't want anyone to see that his eyes were filled with tears, so he left too—through a different door.

Chip ran down the street. "What's wrong with me?" he asked himself out loud. This time, someone answered.

"I think you're dealing with a giant anger," the voice said. Chip looked up. It was his dad! "Come with me, Son," Cliff said.

They walked to a nearby park. Chip still felt full of anger. He didn't like the feeling. It scared him.

They were quiet for a few minutes. Then Chip asked, "What did you mean when you said, 'giant anger,' Dad?"

"Chip, lately you seem angry at everybody—Nuggie, your friends, even your mom and me. It's like your anger is a giant that has gotten a hold of you."

Chip thought about that for a minute. He did realize that his anger was out of control. "What can I do?"

"Sometimes when I get angry a lot at everybody," Cliff said, "I know that I'm really only angry at one person."

"Who?" Chip asked.

"Me. When I don't like myself or I know I'm doing something wrong, I have a really hard time being kind and forgiving to others."

Chip and Cliff talked for a while. And even though Chip's anger didn't totally go away, he realized that his anger was a sign that he needed to talk to God about what was in his heart. After his dad left, Chip sat in the park a long time. "God," he said. "I get so angry when things don't go just like I want them to. Help me to be patient with others—and myself."

The next day, he came home from school and Nuggie ran up to him with big tears in her eyes. "Chip," she said, "please don't be mad. I forgot to feed Ruff again!"

For a minute Chip felt himself getting really angry. Then he looked at Nuggie. He saw how sad she was—and how scared she was of him. "That's OK, Nuggie," he said. "I fed him this morning. I don't want you to worry about it anymore."

"You mean, you're not mad at me?" she asked.

"Not at all," Chip said.

Thinkin' It Through!

* Why do you think Chip got so angry?

* What helped him?

* Think about the last time you were angry. How could you have handled things differently?

BULLSEYE'S ON-TARGET TALK

★ THINK BEFORE YOU SPEAK: God will help you!

Anger can be kind of a scary feeling, can't it? Sometimes anger can make you feel out of control! Being angry isn't necessarily wrong. Even God gets angry when people sin. But most of us get angry when things just don't go our way. Maybe you want to wear a certain shirt to school, but it's in the dirty clothes, so you get mad at your parents for not doing your laundry. Or maybe you made a bad grade on a test, so you get mad at your teacher for making the test too hard.

Sometimes anger is just a way to avoid the real problem: your own responsibility. Is it really your teacher's fault that you didn't do well? Or is it because you didn't study enough?

Maybe you get mad sometimes and you know that you shouldn't, but you just can't stop yourself. God knows how hard it is to take back angry words you say. You really can't take them back, can you?

If you say something mean to someone, even if you apologize, you still said it.

That's why it's important to remember James 1:19: "Everyone should be quick to listen, slow to speak and slow to become angry." If you think about why you're upset before yelling or stomping out of the room, you may be able to calm down and feel better sooner.

SET IN STONE: Bullseye's Memory Verse

Everyone should be quick to listen, slow to speak and slow to become angry. *James 1:19*

GET ROCKIN'
HOW CAN YOU TAME THE ANGER GIANT?
CHECK THESE OUT!

✳ What makes you angry? Do you get angry because someone else did something wrong? Or because you did?

✳ The next time you start to feel angry, take three deep breaths before you say anything. This may help you be "slower" in getting angry!

✳ If someone in your life really frustrates you and angers you, try saying a prayer for that person. Ask God to help you to love that person, even when they do wrong things.

CHAPTER 6

NUGGIE SPELLS TROUBLE

But I trust in your unfailing love; my heart rejoices in your salvation.
Psalm 13:5

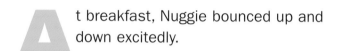

At breakfast, Nuggie bounced up and down excitedly.

"Nuggie, dear, be careful," her mom said. "You'll spill your Rock-Os!"

"I can't help it, Mom," Nuggie answered. "The spelling bee is today! I know I can win."

"Are they still doing spelling bees?" asked Chip. "I went to the regional bee when I was your age."

Ruby said, "You'll do a great job, but I'm sure other rocks will try to win, too."

"But none of them has a chance!" Nuggie said. "I know all the rules like 'I before E expect after C.'"

"Come on, Nuggie," Chip said. "We'll be late for school."

Nuggie's teacher was surprised by how distracted Nuggie seemed. She couldn't solve the math problem, she forgot her geography homework, and she didn't touch her lunch.

"What has gotten into you, Nuggie?" her teacher asked. All Nuggie did was mutter, "I before E" under her breath.

At last school was over. Nuggie ran to the gym where the spelling bee was to be held. Mrs. Crag was already there, telling people where to stand.

"You should put me in the front of the line," said Nuggie. "I know I'll win!"

Lots of other rocks from Nuggie's class were there, too. The spelling bee was a big deal. Nuggie was sad for all the rocks who would be disappointed when she won.

Finally, Mrs. Crag called things to order. "Remember, there can be only one winner. But I hope those of you who don't win will be sure to cheer our champion at the regional spelling bee!"

Then the spelling bee began. Mrs. Crag would read a word for each contestant who repeated it, spelled it, then repeated it again. If any rock forgot to repeat the word or spelled the word incorrectly, that rock was out of the competition.

Nuggie spelled her first word correctly. By the time it was her turn again, many rocks had left the stage. Finally, it was down to Nuggie and Amber. Mrs. Crag turned to Nuggie and said, "Inconceivable."

Nuggie took a deep breath. "Inconceivable," she said. "I-N-C-O-N-C-I oh, I mean E!" But it was too late. Nuggie had spelled the word wrong. "Take a seat, Miss Livingstone," said Mrs. Crag.

Later, Nuggie told her mom and Chip the whole story. "I messed up on the easiest rule! I ran off the stage and Amber won instead! I'm a total failure."

"Come on, Nuggie," said Chip. "At least you'll get to cheer for her at regionals!"

"Only failures do that!" Nuggie said, and she ran to her room.

"I should go talk to her," Ruby said.

"No, Mom," Chip said. "Let me."

Chip found Nuggie lying across her bed. "Go away," she said. "You don't want to talk to a failure like me."

"Nuggie, I know you didn't win. But no one—even you—is the very best at everything. We all fail sometimes."

"Not you," she said to Chip. "You have a band, everyone likes you, and you went to regionals. You weren't a big loser like me."

"Actually, Nuggie, I did lose the spelling bee," Chip said.

"But you said you went to regionals!" Nuggie said.

"I did! I went to cheer on the winner. I didn't know him very well at the time, but now he's one of my best friends."

"Who?" Nuggie asked.

"Splinter! So you see, even though I lost the spelling bee, I made a great friend."

"What happened? Why didn't you win the spelling bee?"

"I fainted," Chip answered.

"You fainted!"

"Right there on stage," he said. "Mrs. Crag had to pour cold water on my head to wake me up." Chip thought for a minute. Then he said, "You know what, Nuggie? I think the most important thing is remembering that God made us and has something important for all of us to do. He sometimes just has different ideas in mind than we do."

"I guess God's ideas are probably better than mine," Nuggie said.

"That's for sure!" Chip said, laughing.

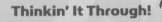

! Thinkin' It Through!

* Why did Nuggie think she would win the spelling bee?

* How did she feel when she didn't win?

* What would you have told Nuggie to help her feel better?

BULLSEYE'S ON-TARGET TALK

★ **TRUST GOD:** He loves you as you are!

No one likes to fail. There's nothing fun about trying to do something and not being able to do it. On the other hand, it's pretty hard to do anything new or better if you are afraid to fail. You probably don't remember when you learned to walk, but you fell down a lot before you could walk on your own. What if you'd stopped trying the first time you fell? You might still be crawling!

Life will always be like that. You will try to do things. Sometimes you'll get them right away, but sometimes you will fail. Guess what? God loves you even when you fail! In fact, some of the most important people in the Bible were "failures." Adam and Eve were the first people to sin, but God still allowed them to be the father and mother of all people. Joseph was a slave, but God put him in a place to be in charge of almost all of Egypt. Paul was hurting Christians, but God gave him another chance and Paul went on to write most of the New Testament!

In the same way, God can use you just as you are. He doesn't want you to be discouraged when you fail. He just wants you to rely on him. Others can see God's power even more clearly when they know he's working in you and through you. And remember, God's love will never fail!

SET IN STONE: Bullseye's Memory Verse

My grace is sufficient for you, for my power is made perfect in weakness. *2 Corinthians 12:9*

GET ROCKIN'
RISE ABOVE THE FAILURE GIANT!
START HERE!

✱ When have you "failed"? Think about the times you've failed and how you responded. What do you wish you'd done differently?

✱ If there is something you've been afraid to do because you thought you might fail, talk to God about helping you give it a try.

✱ Write the memory verse on a card. Put it in your book bag or pocket. Look at it whenever you think you have "failed."

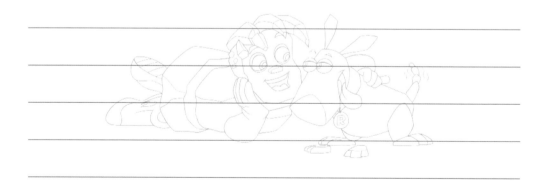

CHAPTER 7

NO TOMATOES, PLEASE!

Cast your cares on the Lord and he will sustain you. Psalm 55:22

"One, two, three, four," Carb counted for the start of the song, but nothing happened.

Gem, Chip, Carb, and Splinter were supposed to be rehearsing for their next concert. The God Rocks! had been asked to play in nearby Granitville, and they were a little nervous.

"Hey, are you guys cracked?" Carb asked. "Why aren't you playing?"

"Uh, sorry Carb," said Chip. "I couldn't remember the intro."

"Yeah," said Gem. "And I forgot the words."

"What? We've played that song a million times," Carb said. "Let's try it again. One, two, three, four . . ."

Again, nothing happened. "What is it *this* time?" Carb asked.

"My throat feels all gravel-y," Gem said.

"I broke a string," Chip said.

"My amp's turned down," Splinter said.

"What's really wrong, guys?" Carb asked.

Gem had big tears in her eyes when she said, "It's, it's just that . . . we've never played in Granitville before."

"Yeah," said Splinter. "What if they think we're just a bunch of dumb pebbles?"

"Granitville is a lot bigger than Rocky Ridge," said Chip. "They might boo us."

"Or throw rotten tomatoes at us," said Splinter.

"Or walk out!" wailed Gem.

"You guys are right," said Carb. "I bet nobody will even come to see us, anyway."

Rehearsal was over, even though the concert was just two days away. And things weren't any better at school the next day. When Mrs. Crag asked Gem to name the rock who founded Rocky Ridge, she muttered, "That's too hard of a question for a dumb rock like me."

"But, Gem, the street you live on is named after him!" Mrs. Crag said, surprised.

"Oh, yeah," Gem said. "That's right."

Chip and Carb both lost their rocketball games in gym. Splinter didn't even go to class; he just sat in front of his locker with his

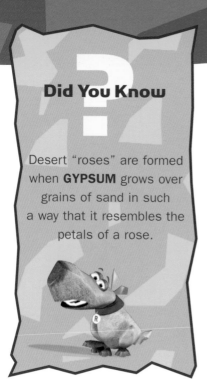

Did You Know

Desert "roses" are formed when **GYPSUM** grows over grains of sand in such a way that it resembles the petals of a rose.

bass at his side. "I'm not good enough to play you," he whispered to it.

That night the band got together for their last practice before the concert, but none of them was in a good mood. "Maybe we should cancel the concert," Gem said.

"Now WAIT a second, rocks!" Chip said. "I know we're all nervous, but The God Rocks! do NOT cancel concerts!"

"We did one time!" said Carb.

"That's because there was a blizzard!" Chip said. "The National Rock Guard said that no rocks were to leave home! *That* was a little different."

"But Chip," Gem said. "They'll *hate* us in Granitville."

"First of all," said Chip, "you don't know that they'll hate us. And SECOND of all, we don't play our music so that people will like us!"

"We *don't?*" asked Carb, Splinter, and Gem.

"No!" Chip said. "We play our music to praise God! Remember? If the world won't yell it out, we, the rocks will cheer and shout! It's great if everyone enjoys our music, but we play it to please God."

"I know, Chip, but my voice just isn't good enough . . ." Gem said.

Chip thought for a minute. "I don't think God cares how well we sing or play, if we're giving him our best," he said.

"Chip, you're right," said Splinter. "We can't let anything stop us from doing what God wants us to do."

"Then what are we waiting for?" asked Carb. "One, two, three, four . . ."

Even after Chip's pep talk, they were all still a little nervous. Right before the concert, they got together to pray.

"Dear God," said Carb. "Please help us to play our best tonight."

"And give praise to you," said Chip.

"And please don't let them throw things at us," said Gem.

The lights went up, and the show began. And The God Rocks!— rocked. They played better than they ever had! Soon the crowd was standing and clapping. But then . . .

"Hey!" said Gem. "Someone just threw something at me!" She looked pretty upset.

"Look, Gem," Chip said. "It's not a rotten tomato—it's a rose!"

And the band played on.

Thinkin' It Through!

* Why do you think the band felt so nervous and insecure about the concert?

* What did Chip say that helped them?

* When do you feel nervous or insecure?

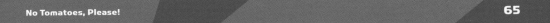

BULLSEYE'S ON-TARGET TALK

★ **GOD MADE YOU:** You are an important part of the body.

Even though Chip, Gem, Carb, and Splinter had been playing together for a long time, they still got nervous about their concert. Why? Because they were insecure. They didn't feel confidence in their ability to play the music.

Lots of us feel insecure sometimes. We feel like we're not good enough, that people don't like us much, that we aren't dressed in the right kind of clothes, that we're not smart enough. You may look at someone else and think, "I wish I could sing like her" or "I wish I was as funny as him."

But God made you to be YOU, not someone else. We've all been given different gifts. The Bible compares Christians to a body, and each Christian is a different body part. One might be a nose, another a foot, another an elbow. The elbow might say, "I'd much rather be a nose." But what if every part wanted to be a nose?

Then who would hear? And see? And walk? Each Christian is given different abilities so that we can all work together. Some of those abilities seem more "important" than others. You might think that the preacher is more important than the person who vacuums the church. But God sees all the jobs as important, and he's happy when each of us is doing what he created us to do.

When we feel badly about our abilities, it's like telling God that he messed up when he made us. But the Bible says that each person is "fearfully and wonderfully made" (Psalm 139:14). God is pleased when you serve him with whatever gifts you have. So don't feel bad about who you are—after all, God made you!

SET IN STONE: Bullseye's Memory Verse

I praise you because I am fearfully and wonderfully made.

Psalm 139:14

GET ROCKIN'
WANT TO DEFEAT THE INSECURITY GIANT? HERE'S HOW!

★ The next time you feel insecure, ask God to show you what he created you to do!

★ Read 1 Corinthians 12:12–27. These verses talk about how we're all a part of one body. Which part do you think you are?

★ Make a list of the things you are insecure about. Pray to God and ask him to help you understand why he created you the way he did. You may never understand all the reasons, but you can be sure that God does!

CHAPTER 8

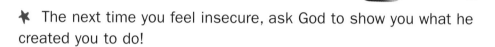

MRS. CRAG'S BIG SECRET

*A gossip betrays a confidence, but a trustworthy man
keeps a secret.* Proverbs 11:13

Kitney Stoon stood in front of her locker, trying once again to remember her combination.

"Oh, no!" she heard Mrs. Crag say from the nearby teacher's lounge. "If they find me, I'm going to be in big trouble!" Kitney stood there, spinning her lock, trying to imagine what might be wrong.

"Forget your combination *again?*" Crystal asked. She and her best friend, Twinkee, had lockers near Kitney's.

"Maybe you should have the combination engraved on your hand, Kitney," said Twinkee, laughing.

Kitney's cheeks turned ruby red. So that Crystal and Twinkee would leave her alone, she told them what she'd just heard. "I just heard Mrs. Crag in the teacher's lounge, and she sounded really upset."

The plan worked. Crystal and Twinkee forgot about Kitney's lock. "Do you think they caught her stealing snacks from the vending machine?" Crystal asked.

"Or maybe she's got a secret identity that's just been discovered, and she's got to leave the school in shame," guessed Twinkee.

"Maybe she's, like, a criminal, and she is about to get sent to jail!" Crystal suggested.

Kitney felt bad, but the two most popular rocks in school didn't usually talk to her.

"Thanks for the scoop, Kit," Crystal said.

"You won't tell anybody else, will you?" Kitney asked, suddenly feeling a little worried. "I didn't really hear much, and I don't know what it meant."

"Don't worry," said Crystal with a smile. "We won't tell a *rock*." She and Twinkee both walked away, giggling.

Oh, well, thought Kitney. *As long as they don't tell anyone else . . .*

At lunchtime, the cafeteria was even noisier than usual. Kitney passed Mrs. Crag and smiled at her. Mrs. Crag smiled back. *Her smile is a little creepy,* thought Kitney.

She sat at her usual table with Gem. "Did you hear about Mrs. Crag?" Gem asked. "She is in big trouble."

"I know," said Chip, who had just walked up with Carb and Splinter, "she's a criminal!"

"I heard she held up a bank," Carb said.

"Our lives are in danger!" said Splinter.

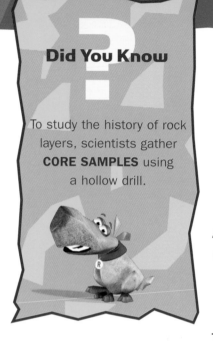

Kitney was miserable, but she was too embarrassed to admit the truth.

That afternoon there was an all-school assembly to kick off Rock History Month. The students all seemed a little nervous. After all, what if Mrs. Crag really was a criminal?

"We're here today to begin our celebration of Rock History Month," Mrs. Crag began, but she didn't get any further.

Twinkee stood up and said, "We don't want to learn about rock history from some criminal!"

Mrs. Crag looked shocked. Kitney could tell that the rumors weren't true. Mrs. Crag didn't have any idea what Twinkee was talking about. "What is going *on?*" she asked. Suddenly the room got very quiet. It was as if, all at once, the students knew how silly it was to think that Mrs. Crag was a criminal. Mrs. Crag looked at Twinkee. "Why do you think I'm a criminal?" she asked.

"Kitney Stoon told me so, ma'am," Twinkee said.

"Miss Stoon, come to my office," said Mrs. Crag.

When they sat down, they were both quiet for a long time. Finally, Kitney said, "I never said you were a criminal, Mrs. Crag."

"I didn't think you did, dear," she answered.

"But . . ." said Kitney, wanting to be totally honest, "I did tell Crystal and Twinkee about what you said in the teacher's lounge about being in trouble."

Mrs. Crag started to chuckle. "Oh, Kitney," she said. "I found out that I've had 10 parking tickets! I knew that if the police saw my car in the wrong spot again, I'd be in trouble. So I went to move my car."

"I'm so sorry, Mrs. Crag!" she said.

"I know you didn't mean any harm, dear. But that's how gossip goes. It can start well enough, but misunderstandings and too much imagination can make gossip get out of control, and eventually, someone innocent could get hurt. That's why God tells us not to do it."

Then Mrs. Crag smiled. This time Kitney thought her smile was *perfect*.

! Thinkin' It Through!

* How did the gossip about Mrs. Crag get started?

* Why did the gossip spread so much?

* What do you do when you hear gossip?

BULLSEYE'S ON-TARGET TALK

★ **HONOR GOD:** Build others up.

You may have heard that gossip is wrong. But what is gossip? Gossip is information that gets passed from person to person. Usually gossip says something bad about someone else. And gossip isn't spread so that person can be helped, but so that other people can look down on or make fun of that person.

Sometimes gossip can be true—the facts are right—but the heart of the person spreading the gossip isn't loving. Most of the time, though, gossip isn't true, at least not all the way, and it's hard to tell where the truth stops and the lies begin. Think about it. If each person who retells the story just adds one little detail that isn't totally true, by the time five or six people have told it, there may not be any truth to it at all!

If anyone has ever gossiped about you, you know how much it hurts. Usually no one will tell you what the gossip is about, but people might whisper when you walk by, laugh at you, or ignore you.

The Bible says some strong things about gossip. Romans 1:28–30 lists all kinds of evil things that people do, things like murder, lying, and hating God. But guess what else is in that list? Gossip! God thinks gossip is a very serious thing.

Remember that it takes two to gossip: one to tell the story, and the other to listen and spread it. Gossip is hurtful and not something that makes God happy.

SET IN STONE: Bullseye's Memory Verse

Do not let any unwholesome talk come out of your mouths, but only what is helpful for building others up.

Ephesians 4:29

GET ROCKIN'
NEED HELP TAMING THE GOSSIP GIANT? CHECK THESE OUT!

✸ The next time you want to tell a friend a story about someone else, ask yourself if you'd want that story told about you. And the next time someone tries to tell you a gossipy story, don't listen, and don't pass it on!

✸ Instead of spreading gossip, think of kind, encouraging words you can say to people.

✸ If you hear a story about someone that seems really serious, either talk to that person or to an adult you trust.

CHAPTER 9

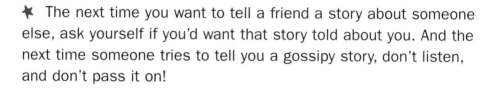

THE DONUTS MADE ME DO IT!

Because he himself suffered when he was tempted, he is able to help those who are being tempted. Hebrews 2:18

Chip's dad walked into the kitchen, checking over his shoulder to make sure no one was watching . . .

"Cliff!" his wife, Ruby said.

"AHHH!!" Cliff yelled. "You scared me!"

"What are you doing, dear?" Ruby asked.

"Um, nothing, sugar rock," Cliff replied.

"You were about to eat another Crunchy Crisp donut, weren't you? You remember what Dr. Wellrock said about eating so many donuts, don't you?"

Cliff nodded. "I just need to throw them away," he said. "It's too tempting to have them in the house."

"That's a good idea," said Ruby. "I won't buy them anymore, either. Although the kids may be upset."

"Upset about what?" Chip asked as he walked in the room, yawning.

"I'm not going to buy anymore Crunchy Crisp donuts," his mom said.

Chip grumbled, but didn't complain too much. He had other things on his mind. He hadn't shown his mom and dad his latest report card, and they were supposed to sign it before he took it to school today.

"Is something on your mind, dear?" his mom asked him.

Chip thought for a minute. Then he said, "I just wanted to tell you that, um, you're the greatest mom ever."

Ruby smiled.

"Chicken!" said Nuggie, as she and Chip started out the door for school.

"Be sure to keep your coat on, dear!" Ruby said to Nuggie.

"OK, Mom," Nuggie answered. But as soon as they got outside, Nuggie took her coat off and stuffed it in her backpack.

"But you just told Mom that you'd keep it on!" Chip said.

"And you just DIDN'T tell Mom about your grades!" Nuggie answered. Neither of them said another word until they got to the bus stop.

When Chip got on the bus, he sat next to Carb. "Hey," he said. "Sign my report card for me."

But Carb didn't want to. "I'm not sure about this, bud."

When Chip turned his report card in to Mrs. Crag, he hoped she wouldn't notice there wasn't a signature. She looked at it closely. "What did your parents say when you showed them your report card?" she asked.

"Not much," Chip said. At least that was close to the truth!

"Alright, have a seat, it's time for class to begin," she said.

When Chip got home from school, he went to the garage to get his bike. Cliff was there, too. "DAD!" he yelled. Cliff was pulling donuts out of his toolbox. "What are you doing?"

His dad looked up, embarrassed. "I, uh, I . . ."

"You're eating those donuts, aren't you?" Chip asked.

Ruby walked in. "Dad's been hiding donuts!" Chip said.

"Then I guess he's not the only one hiding something. We all need to have a talk." Chip hadn't seen his mom this red in a long time. She must be really mad!

"Chip, Nuggie, do you know what the word 'temptation' means?"

"It's when you want to do something you shouldn't do," Nuggie said.

"That's right. And all of us are tempted. But when we give into that temptation—when we do the thing we know we shouldn't— that's when we are doing something wrong."

"Like dad eating those donuts," Chip said. He and Nuggie both giggled.

"Yes, but it's also like when you decide not to tell us about your report card. Or when Nuggie takes her coat off after I've told her to keep it on," Ruby said. Chip and Nuggie stopped giggling.

"But I was hot!" Nuggie said.

"And it just seemed so much easier not to tell you," Chip said. "I knew I could get my grades up for the next time."

"Both of you took the easy way out instead of the right way. And the easy way may seem like a good choice, but in the long run, the right way is the only right choice to make."

"I guess we've all been making some bad decisions," Cliff said. "The good thing is that we can get a clean start. Let's start making good decisions—right now."

"You got it, Dad," Chip and Nuggie said.

Thinkin' It Through!

* Why was Chip tempted to be dishonest about his report card?

* How did Chip, Nuggie, and Cliff each give in to temptation?

* What do you do when you are tempted?

BULLSEYE'S ON-TARGET TALK

★ **GOD WILL PROTECT YOU:** Look to him for help!

Do you ever feel like you really want to do something wrong? Like you just can't stop yourself? Sometimes, when people do wrong things, they say, "the devil made me do it." But the Bible says that God will not allow us to be tempted beyond what we can handle (1 Corinthians 10:13). Other people may try to tempt you into doing things you know are wrong, or your own heart and mind may want to take the "easy way out" by lying or cheating. But you are the one who is responsible for those choices. You can't blame God or the devil or your friends.

So what do you do when you feel tempted? For one thing, even realizing that you *are* feeling tempted to do wrong is a good thing. That means you know in your heart what God says is right, and the Holy Spirit is telling you that what you are about to do is wrong.

When you feel tempted, don't be afraid. Tell God about it. Ask him to give you wisdom and strength to make good choices. Sometimes, though, you are going to make bad choices anyway. When you do, talk to God about that, too. Because Jesus died on the cross to pay for your sins, God will forgive you when you do wrong if you ask him to.

SET IN STONE: Bullseye's Memory Verse

The Lord is faithful, and he will strengthen and protect you from the evil one.   *2 Thessalonians 3:3*

GET ROCKIN'
WANT TO STAND STRONG AGAINST THE TEMPTATION GIANT? HERE ARE SOME IDEAS!

✸ What kinds of things do you often feel tempted to do? Lie to your parents? Disobey your teachers? Say mean things to your friends? Think about what tempts you most often, and talk to God about that. Ask him to remind you that what you are about to do is wrong *before* you do it and give you strength to stop.

✸ If there are certain people in your life who like to persuade you to do wrong things, avoid those people and situations.

✸ Each night before you go to bed, talk to God. Give him praise and thanks, but also tell him about the wrong things you've done that day, and ask him to forgive you.

CHAPTER 10

THE TIMES ARE A-CHANGING

"I am the Alpha and the Omega," says the Lord God, "who is, and who was, and who is to come, the Almighty." Revelation 1:8

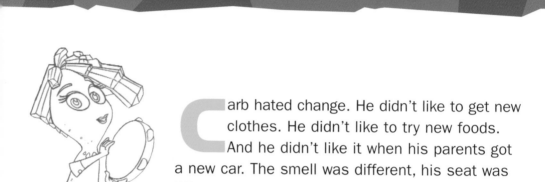

Carb hated change. He didn't like to get new clothes. He didn't like to try new foods. And he didn't like it when his parents got a new car. The smell was different, his seat was different, *everything* was different. And for Carb, different was bad.

But he especially hated when people changed.

When his mom got a haircut—well, Carb didn't sleep for a week.

For a while, Carb didn't experience very many changes. He always bought the same brand of drumsticks (although he didn't like it when he had to get new ones), and he'd had the same best friends for a long time.

Then one day . . .

"Hey, Carb!" Chip said. "I have new music for you to look at."

Carb started to squirm. "Whoa! New music?" he asked. "Well, OK . . ." New music wasn't so bad. He got nervous, and he practiced really hard, but he knew he couldn't be in a band and not play any new music. Besides, some of the new songs had become his favorites.

At lunch, Gem couldn't stop smiling. "Guess what? I just heard from the Lapis Lazuli Vocal Music Workshop. You know, the one I auditioned for? Anyway, instead of just wanting me to come for a week of camp, Miss Lazuli has asked me to come for the whole summer!"

"Wow, Gem," Chip said. "That's great! What will you do?"

"I'll go to the workshop," she said, "but I'll also help some of the younger pebbles!"

"You love working with pebbles," Splinter said. "You'll have a blast!"

"It will mean being away from Rocky Ridge all summer, though," Gem said. "And I'll really miss you rocks. Promise you'll write me?"

"Sure!" Splinter and Chip said. Carb was quiet.

After a minute, Carb said, "But what about the band?"

"Oh!" Gem said. "I was so excited, I hadn't thought about that. I won't be able to do any concerts this summer."

"But we *always* do concerts in the summer!" Carb said.

Chip was a little concerned, too, but he said, "It's OK, Carb. We'll work something out."

"But it won't be the same!" Carb yelled and left the table.

After dinner that night, his mom said, "Carb, your father and I have decided to look into buying a new house."

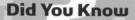

Did You Know

Ocean shores are ever changing as the surf pounds away at the cliffs, leaving arches, caves, and pillars of rock called **SEA STACKS**.

"What?!" Carb said. "We can't move! What about school? And all my friends?"

"We're not leaving Rocky Ridge," said his dad. "We're just moving to a new house. Now that your brother and sister have moved out, we don't need this much room."

"But this is MY house!" Carb said. "I've always lived here. I don't want another rock sleeping in my room."

Carb went to his room. *Why does everything have to change?* he said to himself as he slammed the door behind him.

His dad knocked on the door. "Can I come in?"

"I guess," Carb said.

"Carb," his dad said, "I know you're upset. And I understand. I don't like change much either. But a wise old rock once said, 'The only thing you can count on for sure is change.'"

"What does *that* mean?" Carb asked. His dad was always telling him what some wise rock had said. Carb wished that wise rock hadn't talked so much.

"It just means that change is going to happen. As much as we might not like it, we can't stop it. You're changing all the time.

You're growing up. Before long you'll be done with school. You might get a job. Have a family. Who knows? But things won't stay like they are—they just can't."

"Even if it's true," Carb said, "I still don't have to like it."

"The wise rock was wrong about one thing, though," his dad said.

His dad had never said the wise rock was wrong before.

"There is someone who NEVER changes—God. He is the same today as he was yesterday and will be forever."

"Really?" Carb asked.

"Yeah. So when the changes in your life seem too hard to handle, go to him. You can always count on him to be the same."

"Dad," Carb said. "I think you're a lot smarter than that wise old rock."

His dad winked, said, "Good night," and turned out the light.

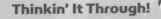

! Thinkin' It Through!

* Why does change bother Carb so much?

* What advice would you have given Carb?

* How do you feel when something in your life changes?

BULLSEYE'S ON-TARGET TALK

★ **GOD NEVER CHANGES:** You can count on it!

There's nothing right or wrong about change in itself. Some changes are good, and some aren't. But most people get a little nervous about changes. After all, you're more comfortable with what you know, right? Your school, your house, your friends—they may not be perfect, but at least you're used to them. That's why things like moving, getting a new teacher, or starting a new sport can be so scary. You might like the new thing, but how do you know? What if no one likes you? What if you're no good? What if? What if? What if?

The fact is, change is going to happen. And not all the changes will be happy. But usually there isn't much you can do to stop change. Maybe you can make your parents promise to never move, but what if your best friend's mom gets a new job in a different city? Many changes that happen are out of your control.

OK, so you may not be in control, but God is! And as Carb's dad said, God's the one thing that NEVER changes. He was the same at the beginning of time as he will be at the end, because he's already there! He's eternal!

And he makes a promise to those who believe in him and obey him. He says that he can work all things together for good. Does that mean everything will be good? No! But it does mean that God can bring good from every situation, even bad ones.

So when a change comes around, talk to God about it. Ask him to give you his peace. And know that no matter what changes in your life, you can always count on him!

SET IN STONE: Bullseye's Memory Verse

We know that in all things God works for the good of those who love him, who have been called according to his purpose. *Romans 8:28*

GET ROCKIN'
HERE ARE SOME THINGS TO HELP YOU HANDLE THE CHANGE GIANT!

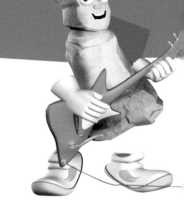

✶ Think about a time when something changed for you. Did you move? Start a new grade? Try a new activity? What happened? How did you feel at first? How did you feel later?

✶ Write a story or paint a picture about something that is going to change in your life. Imagine what that change might be like.

✶ Talk to your mom, dad, and other adults about big changes that happened in their lives. How did they deal with those changes? What were they afraid of? What really happened?

GET ROCKIN'

STORIES FEATURING YOUR FAVORITE GOD ROCKS! CHARACTERS WITH NUGGETS OF WISDOM JUST FOR YOU FROM GOD ROCKS! HEROES.

★ ROCKIN' WITH THE RULES
Understanding the Ten Commandments

Who needs rules? We all do! Follow Chip and his friends as they learn to use God's rules to help them make good decisions in tough situations.

24241 *ISBN 0-7847-1127-5*

★ BEYOND A BLAST FROM THE PAST
Discovering why God made you

Are you ready for a cosmic discovery? God made all of creation with a purpose—including you! Join *The God Rocks!* as they find out what God's plan is all about.

24242 *ISBN 0-7847-1355-3*

★ MORE THAN A SPLATBALL GAME
Squaring off with the giants in your life

Have you ever stood nose-to-knee with trouble? We all have! Chip, Gem, Carb, and Splinter experience their share of giants and wind up victorious—and so can you!

24243 *ISBN 0-7847-1457-6*

THE HIPPEST NEW ANIMATED VIDEO SERIES ON THE BLOCK WITH LIFE LESSONS AND BIBLE TRUTHS!

IF ROCKS FROM BIBLE TIMES COULD TALK, WOULD THEY KEEP SILENT ABOUT THE AMAZING EVENTS THEY WITNESSED? NO WAY! THAT'S WHY EVERY GOD ROCKS! HERO HAS SOMETHING IMPORTANT TO SAY!

* **TEN ROCKIN' RULES** *or . . . Wakin' up is hard to do*
  Chip and his friends learn from the Ten Commandment Twins that God gives us rules because he loves us. Join Chip, Gem, Carb, and Splinter on this wild ride full of twists and turns, and you'll wake up to discover Ten Rockin' Rules!
  DVD includes an avalanche of extras: *Blooper gems, interviews with the creators and the band, God Rocks! desktop wallpaper, widescreen option and MORE!*

* **A BLAST FROM THE PAST** *or . . . Anybody got change for a Buck?*
  Has Rocky Ridge been invaded by mutant vegetables from outer space? Join The God Rocks! as they unearth the solution to the alien mystery. Along the way, you'll hear from Buck, a traveling sales rock, who blasts onto the scene and realizes that God created the universe and everything in it with a purpose.
  DVD includes a meteor shower of extras: *"This Is the Day" music video featuring The God Rocks!, "You've Been Searching" music video featuring Sheryl Stacey, samples from the debut music CD, widescreen option and MORE!*

* **SPLATBALL SQUARE-OFF** *or . . . Nose to knee with a defiant giant*
  As the annual splatball championship begins, the Rocky Ridge Rangers are shaking in their shoes! But Bullseye (Mickey Rooney), their coach, is a God Rocks hero who has been face to face with Goliath, a very defiant giant. In the end, The God Rocks! find out that when we look to God, our giants are never as big as they seem.
  DVD includes a ballpark full of extras: *The God Rocks! Cry Out tour highlights, interviews, games, and MORE!*

VHS 24214 UPC 7-07529-24214-9
DVD 24227 UPC 7-07529-24227-9

VHS 24215 UPC 7-07529-24215-6
DVD 24228 UPC 7-07529-24228-6

VHS 24216 UPC 7-07529-24216-3
DVD 24229 UPC 7-07529-24229-3

Cry Out

SPARKIN' MUSIC THAT'S ENERGIZING, POP-DRIVEN AND CREATED ESPECIALLY FOR KIDS WHO AREN'T AFRAID TO SHOUT "GOD ROCKS!"

✱ CRY OUT

One great new kids' video series, four talented musicians and 14 hot-as-lava songs combine to introduce The God Rocks! in their debut music release, *Cry Out*. The CD features original 10-karat songs of praise and encouragement from the first three episodes of God Rocks! and MORE! Kids will want to sing along with this sparkin' new band as they praise God and give honor to him.

1. This Is the Day
2. God Rules
3. Be Yourself
4. Wonderful Kingdom
5. The Word
6. When God Talks, Creation Rocks
7. You've Been Searching
8. Rocks Cry Out
9. Giant
10. Such a Love
11. Wake Up!
12. Freckle
13. There Is a Place
14. God Rocks!® Theme Song

All songs & music © 2002 Chelsea Road Productions, Inc. (BIGCAR) God Rocks!® and all related characters and elements are trademarks of and copyrighted by Chelsea Road Productions, Inc. All rights reserved. Interior design: Abbott Design. Website: www.godrocksvideo.com.

24261 *UPC 7-07529-24261-3*